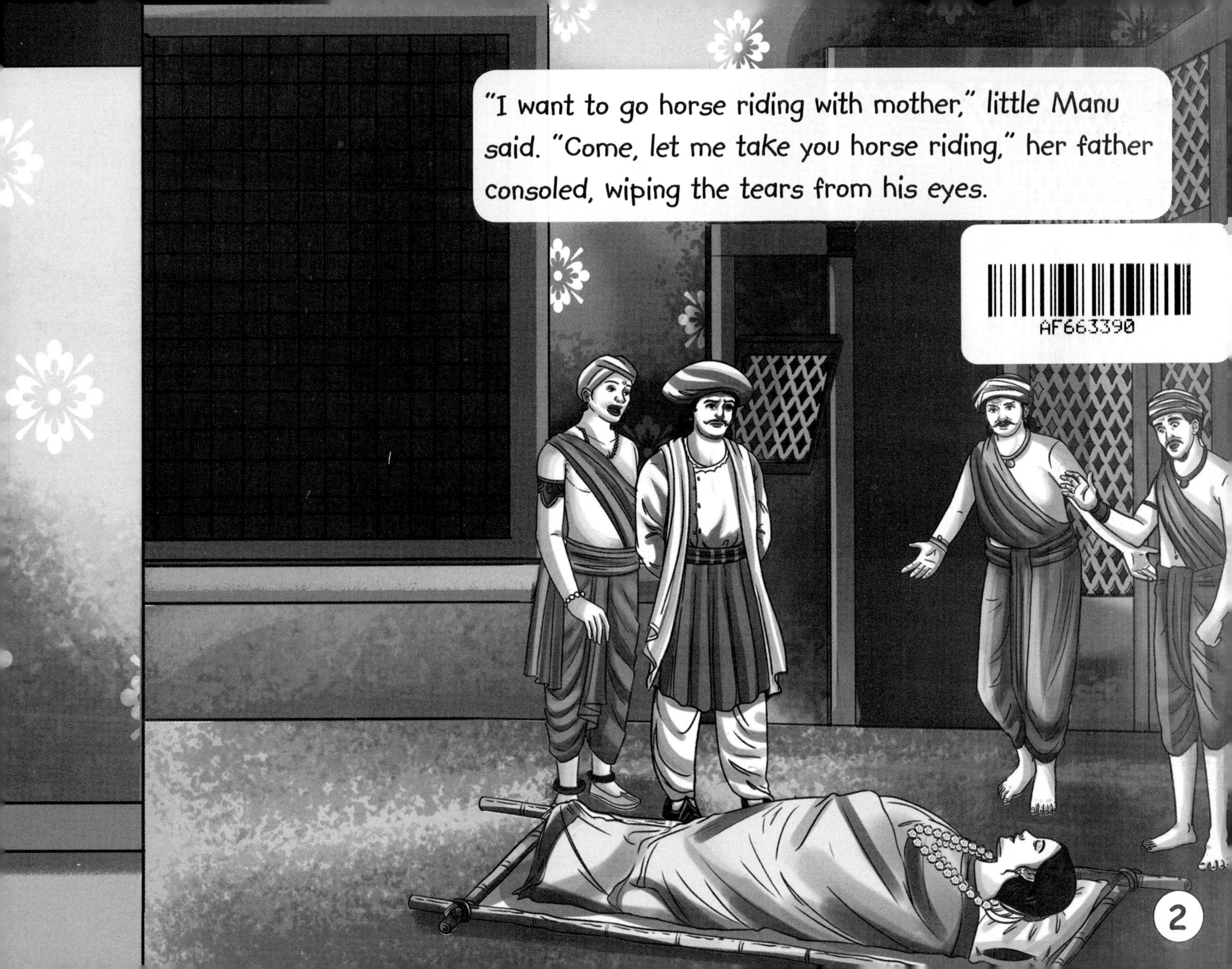

"I want to go horse riding with mother," little Manu said. "Come, let me take you horse riding," her father consoled, wiping the tears from his eyes.

Tambe decided to raise his daughter to become strong and fearless, just as his wife Bhagirathi had wanted. After all, they had named her Manikarnika, after the famous ghat on the banks of the Ganga in Varanasi, where she was born on 19 November, 1827.

He would speak to the Peshwa the next day. She could start learning horse riding, fencing and shooting along with Nana Saheb, the adopted heir to the Peshwa, and his friend Tatya Tope, son of another loyal member of the Peshwa household.

Manu grew up with the boys and she was smarter and cleverer than both of them, despite being younger.

One day, Nana Saheb was riding on an elephant. Manu was excited and wanted to ride it too.

"You can't. This is my elephant," he told her.

"One day I will have 10 elephants for every one of yours," she said and ran into the palace.
Manu was furious. She hated being second to anyone.

Meanwhile, in a village near Jhansi, another little girl was growing up, not knowing how much her story was going to be intertwined with that of Manu. Jhalkari was the daughter of Sadoba Singh, a poor villager. Like Manu, she lost her mother Jamuna Devi early. She grew up with no education, but was taught horse riding and how to use weapons.

Jhalkari was fearless and strong, fighting off dacoits who had attacked her village, and even a tiger with her bare hands.

When Manu was married to the King of Jhansi, Gangadhar Rao, in 1842, she was given the title of Rani Lakshmi Bai.

One day during a festival at the palace, she came across Jhalkari, who was engaged to Puran Singh, a soldier. She was struck by the uncanny resemblance to herself and when she heard how brave Jhalkari was, she recruited her into the women's army.

In 1851, Rani Lakshmi Bai gave birth to a son, but she lost him four months later. The King and queen were grief-stricken.

They decided to adopt a child so that Jhansi would have an heir. In 1853, they adopted Damodar Rao, a distant cousin of the King, as their son in the presence of the British political agent Major Ellis. The next year Gangadhar Rao died.

Governor General Lord Dalhousie, however, refused to accept the adoption, as he wanted to annex Jhansi and make it a part of the East India Company. He used the recently proclaimed Doctrine of Lapse, according to which if a king died without an heir, the kingdom would become part of the British empire.

Rani Lakshmi Bai appealed against Lord Dalhousie's decision. It was rejected, but she continued to appeal till early 1856. "I will never give up my Jhansi," she proclaimed to loud cheers from her people. They promised to join her in protecting Jhansi.

For some time, there had been rumblings of discontent in the British Indian army. In 1856, an act made it compulsory for Indian soldiers to go wherever their British officers sent them. This upset large sections of the army. In addition to this, they had to pull the Enfield gun cartridge plugs with their teeth and it was said that the British had smeared it with cow and pig fat. This angered the Hindu and Muslim soldiers.

On 10 May, 1857 soldiers at the Meerut cantonment refused to operate the Enfield guns. When their British officers insisted, the soldiers revolted. This was the start of the first war of Independence. Rani Lakshmi Bai became one of the heroines of the 1857 war of independence because of her brave defence of Jhansi.

Her army was, however, defeated and she escaped with her son strapped to her back. To give her a head start, Jhalkari dressed like her and fought against Sir Hugh Rose's forces. By the time he realised that he had been duped, Rani Lakshmi Bai had reached the safety of the forces led by Nana Saheb and Tatya Tope.

Rani Lakshmi Bai became one of the heroines of the 1857 war of independence because of her brave defence of Jhansi.

Rani Lakshmi Bai's final battle was in Gwalior when she dressed like a man and fought fiercely against the British. She was badly wounded, but managed to escape from the battlefield. She was found by a sage who took her to his hut, where she died on 18 June, 1857. Before she died she asked the sage to cremate her as she did not want the British to find her body.

On learning of her death, Sir Hugh wrote: "Although she was a lady, she was the bravest and best military leader of the rebels. A man among the mutineers."

NAME YOUR FAVOURITE FREEDOM FIGHTERS

1 ....

2 ....

3 ....

4 ....

5 ....

6 ....

7 ....

8 ....

9 ....

10 ....